What Did Christ Say About Our Troubling Times?

Charles Prettow

What Did Christ Say About Our Troubling Times?
February 2021

ISBN 978-1-943412-17-4

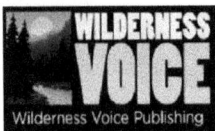

Published by
Wilderness Voice Publishing
PO Box 857
Canon City, CO 81215

"A voice crying in the wilderness –
proclaiming the good news of the coming Kingdom!"

Contents

Noise, Lies and Confusion

Over the last fifty plus years Christians have heard countless theories and interpretations of Scripture concerning how the end-of-this-age will unfold. During this time false prophets and false alarmists have come and gone, declaring dates when Christ will return and many end-time apocalyptic events that never materialized. These are some of the serious reasons why most believers today have become numb to all the signs that Christ warned would take place, pointing to the end. (See Matthew 24:3-8.)

Then there is the false teaching that has added to this numbness; the belief that the rapture will occur before any real trouble comes to the world, particularly to America. Another false teaching, that has helped many believers become indifferent, is that somehow a powerful revival will come and convert a multitude of unbelievers to Christ. This supposed revival or awakening will set America and the world back on the right

4

course and usher in the physical reign of Christ on Earth.

Another lie is that America, as a nation founded on Judeo-Christian principles, will be preserved from any severe trouble—no matter what!

Jesus said, the end would not come all at once: Many Christians, beginning in the mid-seventies expected Christ to return at any moment. Books like The Late Great Planet Earth, by Hal Lindsey in 1970, and later The Left Behind series of books, by Tim LaHaye and Jerry B. Jenkins in the mid-nineties, convinced many Christians they would be raptured anytime, with the belief that God would rescue Christians from all end-time troubles.

Jesus said there would many false prophets and false teachers deceiving many as the end took its time approaching. With the many false prophets and false end-of-the-age teachings mixed with unprecedented prosperity over the last fifty years, most

Christians are sound asleep. All this end-time noise, lies, and confusion has cancelled the reality that the end is now upon us. Christ described this sleepy condition of the last day Christian in the parable of the Ten Maidens. (See Matthew 25:1-13.)

As for the good-hearted lost sinner, and the backslid Christian, the words Mega-Church and corruption became synonymous. With the rise of arrogant flamboyant ministers, numerous sex scandals, and greedy ministries, the Gospel is now maligned by many, just as the Apostle Peter predicted: *"And many will follow their sensuality, and because of them the way of truth will be blasphemed. And in their greed they will exploit you with false words. Their condemnation from long ago is not idle, and their destruction is not asleep"* (2 Peter 2:2-3).

The so-called "Moral Majority" movement within Christianity became a finger pointing crusade against lost sinners and a growing immoral American culture, while downplaying and ignoring the ever-increasing

Christian scandals. When comparing these Christian public disgraces in relationship to the election cycles, it becomes obvious that conservative losses directly correlate to exposed scandals and Christian hypocrisy.

Since the delay of that seventies and nineties awakening to Christ's soon return, the continued American prosperity, and the false teachings, most Christians are unprepared to endure the approaching end-of-this-age troubles. Christ warned of this dangerous condition for the end-time Christian in the parable of the Ten Maidens: *"As the bridegroom was delayed, they all became drowsy and slept"* (Matthew 25:5). Even worse, unprepared Christians in this parable were locked out of eternity.

Few believers take time to study Christ's words for themselves and watch for the end-of-this-age signs that should awaken them and keep them awake. Jesus said the last day's world cultures would become wicked and perverse, just as it was in the days of Noah and Lot—another fulfilled sign.

7

Another huge sign is persecution towards true Christians that has now started, which should be apparent to the sincere believer. We are in a time of hatred that Christ warned of: *"Then they will deliver you up to tribulation and put you to death, and you will be hated by all nations for my name's sake. And then many will fall away and betray one another and hate one another. And many false prophets will arise and lead many astray. And because lawlessness will be increased, the love of many will grow cold. But the one who endures to the end will be saved"* (Matthew 24:9-13). Already the backlash from the far left and liberal Democrats is boiling with hatred towards conservatives, as well as Evangelical, Pentecostal, and Charismatic Christians who supported President Trump, and who support conservativism and cultural righteousness.

Few Christians hear sound doctrine and the expounding of Christ's end-time words: There is a fear in most pulpits that suppresses any call of alarm and warning to what is now upon us. Just as the Apostle Paul warned: *"For the time is coming when people will not* *endure sound teaching, but having itching ears they will accumulate for themselves teachers to suit their own passions, and will turn away from listening to the truth and wander off into myths"* (2 Timothy 4:3-4). Many ministers of the Gospel who realize the end is now upon us have been marginalized or ignored. Some are cowardly and shrink back from warning and equipping their flock, for fear of losing attendance or their leadership position.

Let us look closely at Christ's words concerning the end: Christ explained to his disciples (and to us) when the end would come. First, Jerusalem would be trampled by the Gentiles, where the Jewish people would fall by the sword and be taken captive and dispersed among the nations, and the Jewish Second Temple would be destroyed. That judgment came upon God's people (the Jews) some forty years after Christ prophesied that warning, and that judgment would continue until the times of the Gentiles are fulfilled.

Then Christ explains what to watch for when the times of the Gentiles start to be fulfilled: Jesus said: *"Nation will rise against nation, and kingdom against kingdom. There will be great earthquakes, and in various places famines and pestilences [pandemics]. And there will be terrors and great signs from heaven"* (Luke 21:10-11).

The times of the Gentiles started to come to an end in 1917, when the British government made a public statement (The Balfour Declaration) during the First World War. This pronouncement supported the establishment of a "national home for the Jewish people" in Palestine. Also, during the first world war the first modern pandemic (the Spanish Flu) swept throughout the world.

Following WWI, we see the Roaring Twenties take America's morality towards darkness, then the worldwide Great Depression and famine came, leading into the Second World War where Nazi Germany attempted to destroy the Jewish race. The Holocaust shocked the world into

10

allowing the Jewish people, strewn throughout the world, to make a modern-day exodus to Palestine and in 1948 the nation of Israel was birthed.

American Prosperity a Trap: After WWII, prosperity in America grew in leaps and bounds, along with ever-growing public expressions of sexual deviance and violence. American moral values and the sanctity of life progressively slid into darkness and helped spawn blatant evil, increased crime, as well as corporate and political corruption. The powers of darkness were subtly allowed to weaken every traditional American institutional pillar created to maintain law and order and societal civility. The most important pillar, the Church of America became enamored with prosperity and material wealth, greedy to draw followers by hiring flamboyant leaders. Leadership slowly drifted away from leading by example and making disciples of Christ (who are led by the Holy Spirit)—instead, leadership taught Christians to become purpose driven to fulfill leadership's selfish ambitions.

Birth Pains of the Coming Kingdom: Christ called the turbulent times leading to end-of-this-age "birth pains." These "birth pain" troubles are ever increasing in intensity and frequency worldwide. I grew up in the fifties and sixties, and we rarely heard of earthquakes. Major quakes and volcanic activity are now very frequent. All these troubling events, that Christ warned us to watch for, run parallel to the turbulent challenges and wars that Israel has faced in becoming a secure and established nation in Palestine.

Israel, as a nation is about to be free from the times of the Gentiles: Jerusalem is no longer under Gentile rule. However, the Temple Mount is still under control of the Gentiles. Few Christians heard about or understand the dramatic significance of an event that took place on Monday, December 10th, 2018 in Israel. There was a reenactment of the first daily sacrifice in almost 2,000 years, held at the wailing wall at the Temple Mount. Recreation of the ancient instruments and pieces used in the traditional daily sacrifice were used, these recreations have been made to precise Biblical specifications and are now ready to install, once the Third Temple is constructed.

Yes, the altar for the Third Temple is already prefabricated and ready to be assembled, once there is an agreement that allows the Temple Mount to be used to erect the Jewish Third Temple. Christ warned how the "birth pains" would finally lead to the end. We are told to watch for the abomination performed by the antichrist in the Jewish Holy Place. When the Third Temple is erected, this soon to come event will ignite the Great Tribulation.

Globalism, The Antichrist, The Abomination of Desolation, and the Great Tribulation: The world is racing towards a one-world-order and America took a giant leap towards that reality with the election of Joe Biden and Kamala Harris, along with Democrat control of the House and the Senate. With that win, these new political powers are pressing the American populace to conform to their globalist agenda.

This globalist agenda is dividing America and attacking our freedoms and constitutional rights. This far-left agenda is employing censorship of all opposing voices and spawning hateful persecution which will increase, just as Christ said.

This hatred and persecution will lead many Christians to fall away from Christ. This increasing persecution will act as a vetting process of the household of God. Many shallow on-fire believers, carnal spiritualists, lukewarm and false Christians alike will disavow Christ, *"And then many will fall away and betray one another and hate one another"* (Matthew 24:10). On the bright side, the increased hatred, lawlessness, and persecution will challenge the sincere believer to obtain the grace of God, to work out their salvation in fear and trembling— thus, grow up into salvation and eternal security: *"But the one who endures to the end will be saved. And this gospel of the kingdom* *will be proclaimed throughout the whole world as a testimony to all nations, and then the end will come"* (Matthew 24:13-14). God will allow this growing persecution to train a mighty last day's army that proclaims the good news of the coming kingdom of God, being made ready to be used in the final harvest on the day that God acts.

The Only Good News: In review, Christ's words describe what has now started: *"And there will be signs in sun and moon and stars, and on the earth distress of nations in perplexity because of the roaring of the sea and the waves, people fainting with fear and with foreboding of what is coming on the world. For the powers of the heavens will be shaken"* (Luke 21:25-26).

With ever increasing worldwide trouble, soon the only good news will be the proclamation of the coming kingdom of God and Christ's physical return. This good news will encourage many to wake up, straighten up, and become prepared to confidently endure the coming tribulation. The mature believer will trust God and look forward to the rapture and the millennial reign of Christ on Earth. This proclamation of the coming kingdom will usher in the final awakening, but also create more hatred towards true believers.

The Antichrist Revealed: Indeed, Christ said when the antichrist is revealed, these "birth pain" troubles and persecution would escalate into a *"Great tribulation, such as has not been from the beginning of the world until now, no, and never will be"* (Matthew 24:21). However, this period called the Great Tribulation would be shortened: *"And if those days had not been cut short, no human being would be saved. But for the sake of the elect those days will be cut short"* (Matthew 24:22).

To clear up the matter as to when Christians (who are ready) can expect to be raptured to safety, Christ said this: *"But in those days, after that tribulation, the sun will be darkened, and the moon will not give its light, and the stars will be falling from heaven, and the powers in the heavens will be shaken. And then they will see the Son of Man*

16

*coming in clouds with great power and glory.
And then he will send out the angels and
gather his elect from the four winds, from the
ends of the earth to the ends of heaven"*
(Mark 13:24-27).

Understand this, Christ said that these
troubles will come: *"Upon all who dwell on
the face of the whole earth."* (Luke 21:35).
This includes America.

**Please note: The coming Great Tribulation is
not the wrath of God.** Rather, after the
rapture of all true and ready believers, the
wrath of God will be poured out upon the
world. Study the book of Revelation to gain a
clear picture of just how terrible it will be for
those left in the world after the rapture takes
place. Indeed, as Scripture promises: *"For
God has not destined us for wrath, but to
obtain salvation through our Lord Jesus
Christ"* (1 Thessalonians 5:9; read 1
Thessalonians 5:1-11 for full context.)

Giving up the Love of this Life: Please
understand, as a servant of Christ in full time

ministry, I highly value America, her freedoms and heritage. I served five years in the Marine Corps before being honorably discharged in 1975 to enter Bible College in preparation for ministry. My father was a WWII Navy veteran, where one of his many combat experiences was spending 72 hours in continuous operations putting Marines on the beach during the battle of Peleliu and ferrying the wounded back to hospital ships. All my uncles served our country during the war, and most of my aunts worked in war factories.

However, despite my patriotic loyalty, I am a citizen first and foremost of the soon to come kingdom of God. It was difficult and somewhat sad to let go of my love and concern for America and concentrate on preparing for what is now fast approaching upon the whole world, including America. It is an unfortunate reality that America is leading the world into wickedness, corruption, lawlessness, and shameless sexual perversion.

America has passed the point of no return, where the wicked have finally achieved political control. They will work to gain complete control of our society, but only temporarily. (True Christians get it all back when Christ physically returns.) America is sliding with the rest of the world, towards the antichrist rule.

The coming judgments upon America will make the current administration look foolish because of its inability to give direction or solve the many problems, disasters, and perplexing troubles that are about to befall America and the world. This coming worldwide political chaos and impotency will create a leadership vacuum making way for the antichrist rule.

Then, after the rapture, when the wrath of God falls upon the world, America will suffer terrible destruction as referenced in the book of Revelation: *"Fallen, fallen is Babylon the great! She has become a dwelling place for demons, a haunt for every unclean spirit, a haunt for every unclean bird, a haunt for every unclean and detestable beast. For all nations have drunk the wine of the passion of*

19

her sexual immorality, and the kings of the earth have committed immorality with her, and the merchants of the earth have grown rich from the power of her luxurious living'" (Revelation 18:2-3).

We must let go of any idolatrous love of America and her blessings, looking forward to the coming millennial reign of Christ. For now, we must hold our ground for individual rights, the rule of law and local community safety as best as we can and boldly proclaim the good news of Christ's soon return. We must follow Peter's admonition: *"Since all these things are thus to be dissolved, what sort of people ought you to be in lives of holiness and godliness, waiting for and hastening the coming of the day of God, because of which the heavens will be set on fire and dissolved, and the heavenly bodies will melt as they burn! But according to his promise we are waiting for new heavens and a new earth in which righteousness dwells"* (2 Peter 3:11-13).

Find and Attend a Fellowship that Will Help Equip You: My hope is that this article has stirred and inspired you to find solid fellowship and get connected with like-minded believers. If you are not a believer, I encourage you to seek Christ, turn away from sin, and become a believer and a member of God's army, learning to be equipped for life and ministry in these last days. Soon, many will want to hear how to become ready, so it is important that the sincere Christian become effective in sharing the gospel (good news) of the coming kingdom.

Contact Information

You can contact the author by the following:

Mail: MC Global Ministries
        Charles Pretlow
        PO Box 857
        Canon City, CO 81215

Phone: (719) 285-8542

Email: contact@mcgmin.com

Charles is available as a guest speaker. His extensive background in ministry, counseling, and end-of-this-age issues provides sound instruction on overcoming the last-days troubles and wounds to the personal spirit and damaged emotions.

More About the Author

Pastor Charles Pretlow is one of the founders of MC Global Ministries and Wilderness Voice Publishing. Charles began his ministerial work in 1974 and shares insights gained from years of study, ministry, and counseling Christians who struggled in their walk with Christ. He shares sound teachings to help equip the sincere Christian and those in leadership to effectively minister in these dark days leading to Christ's return. Charles' theology is practical, founded in years of experience and training in the discipline of the Lord.

www.ingramcontent.com/pod-product-compliance
Lightning Source LLC
Chambersburg PA
CBHW070756050426
42449CB00010B/2498